Lance Henson

The missing bead

Lance Henson

The missing bead

Poems for the Cheyenne

JustFiction Edition

Imprint
Any brand names and product names mentioned in this book are subject to trademark, brand or patent protection and are trademarks or registered trademarks of their respective holders. The use of brand names, product names, common names, trade names, product descriptions etc. even without a particular marking in this work is in no way to be construed to mean that such names may be regarded as unrestricted in respect of trademark and brand protection legislation and could thus be used by anyone.

Cover image: Author

Publisher:
JustFiction! Edition
is a trademark of
International Book Market Service Ltd., member of OmniScriptum Publishing Group
17 Meldrum Street, Beau Bassin 71504, Mauritius

Printed at: see last page
ISBN: 978-613-9-42732-1

Preface

A Dog Soldier in Exile

> *One of the best contemporary poets in Native America, he is also a partaker in the spiritual life of his Tsistsistas (Southern Cheyenne) people, and consequently, he sees his own lyrical work as tied to the function of the oral tradition. (...) Henson is aware of the didactic and moral responsibilities of storytelling, and besides being an outstanding lyrical poet, he is an untiring storyteller, easily bridging the spiritual and ceremonial with the popular and profane* (Hartmut Lutz, 2002)[1].

> *My approach to poetry is very simple: poems are stories. Poems are stories that reflect human experience. And the best poetry expresses or mirrors the relationship between a human being and the forces that surround his or her life* (Lance Henson, 2002)[2].

There are people who live a life that is different and unusual, hovering on the edge, displaced, in 'exile': Lance Henson is one of them.

The double personal experience of the poet, as a Marine fighting in the Vietnam War and as a 'warrior' in defence of his people, exemplifies the condition of the contemporary Native American individual, loaded down and often overwhelmed by the weight of the injustices and betrayals of colonization which have accumulated in the hearts and minds of the indigenous populations of America during the course of more than five centuries. These autobiographical and historical components run like a red thread in his poetic narrative, and gradually expand into a collective and universal testimony. Henson rarely speaks in the first person, but acts rather as the spokesperson of a universe made up of all kinds of animate and inanimate beings linked by true blood ties and real family relationships, such as where the Earth is Mother, the Sky is Father, and the Moon is Grandmother. The idea is that the whole of creation exists in a reciprocal relationship where each part contributes to the wellbeing and support of the other. The role of Lance Henson as a member of the Dog Soldier Society (a Cheyenne Warrior Clan) is to preserve this balance among his people, thereby reinforcing a warrior spirit that has, however, not so much to do with war – though one must remain vigilant -- but that finds its deepest essence in the spirit of protection of the meek and silent who too frequently cannot make their own desperate cries heard. From Oklahoma to Jordan, to Papua New Guinea to Switzerland, to Italy and beyond, the poet's attention is always alert, inclusive, and welcoming towards these 'wretched of the earth'. Not surprisingly, from 1988 to 2006 he was chosen as spokesperson for the Cheyenne people at the United Nations Conference on Indigenous Peoples in Geneva.

---

[1] Lutz, Hartmut, Approaches, Wißner-Verlag, 2002, p. 199.
[2] Henson, Lance, in *Approaches, op. cit.* p. 199.

Such a complex, often personally dramatic life is inevitably reflected in his poetry, though simple and straight forward at first glance, and in his way of life. He is a rare example of a poet who lives 'as a poet', sometimes as a loner, split between America and Europe, sometimes as an affectionate father; sometimes distant, sometimes immersed in another dimension made of memories of alienation, but of humour and tenderness too. You can see him helping shoulder the suffering of others, sharing the thoughts and misfortunes of an outcast, or lecturing on spiritual, literary and socio-political issues in university classrooms. He is always moving, ready to 'fight'and to resist, accustomed like his people to constant changes, and always in search of a place where his wandering 'exile' can finally come to an end.

That is why those who have been so fortunate to have met him, like myself, cannot but share his world view, appreciate his work, and love him.

Mariella Lorusso

A hazed moon over the Slovakian fields
the night cold
stubble fields of corn from last nights fullness
glitter like messaging flowers

I listen to the wind
it is voice of rain and its eyes of sorrowed remembrance

here in this strange land underground
the hair of another age continues to grow

and there I dreamt of a feather in the snow
and a young woman raising her hands against a bomb

four swans fly over the road to Bratislava

and in Cheyenne country it is spring
the familiar sound of war begins in the murmuring
waters

last night on a deserted street in pressov
I searched for your sweet voice
and found a cold wind opening its door
and a broken phone

Slovakia
3.21.03

A partisan poem

Along the Brenta river
the owls are waking
lost in the dark courage that is their calling
here in this autumn wind
there is a whispering of names

The trees in Bassano have grown old
with a sacred trust

Sons and daughters who cannot forget

Their fathers each night
calling from the darkness where
the owls hunt

Peace on their last words

Peace on you

and me

Bassano del Grappa
3 October 2000

All the names for rain have changed
we say the same words
their meaning burns in another place

And the lightning crosses over
in its mirrors of wind

While the trees are burning outside

Trees made of hands reaching toward you

Trees made of songs of rivers of animals of turnings
inside a stone

Trees where crows call toward us in their shimmering
voices

Trees that watch as smoke rises around them

Blinded trees praying for us as we leave them to their
enemies

Dying trees that hold the names of the forgotten
in front of our eyes

august 22,2002
Untere Hueb, Switzerland

As before smoke rises above another river
Screams and heartbreaking farewells
Billowing

Over the bloody map of monstrous boundaries

Here is the single horror of innocents dying

Washita
          Sava
                Hudson

Vihomiv veho

Smoke rising above another river....

Vihomiv veho..look white man
9.12.01

Ancestrals

There are days born so far from each other
Words too sorrowful to know they are words

All their meanings coming back
Without them....

An old memory washing up in the bells of midnight

I search for you
Sitting by the kerosene lamp of forty years now
I have not lost you

I have lost myself....

Here are the things that do not need us
In shadows
Beside us....

It is already yesterday
Moving
Among
The lamps...

Silent rivers full of broken mirrors and faces
Arriving from the wars....

A dream of a tattered red cloth from sand creek
Falling to earth

But whose dream....

All the sorrowed voices falling away
At the edge of the world

At the edge of everything....

To move in open country

To sit in a clear place
To guard life....

(Cheyenne dog soldier prayer)

At the military cemetery hamm

In Luxembourg
For Jack Whiteshield And Roy Larney

In a slow snow storm last December
I found your graves

The white landscape
Undulating in breaking sunlight

The crunching snow beneath our footsteps
The sloping shadows of headstones weaving a
Breathless pattern of goodbye

In beauty i pray for you
In peace i place this cigarette
my relations

In a circling sage wind

I speak your names....

January05
Jack Whiteshield, my uncle, and Roy Larney
served and died in general George Patton' tank core, 1944

Crossing the Vtalva river

I think of little wolf
In the confused distances of America
Casting a prayer so pure

Who chose the ancient belief that the
Sanctity of words
Was better than killing

So many gentle and beautiful people
For whom the stars no longer shine
The moon beyond their silence touching their
Closed eyes

Crossing the Vtalva river
I remember sweet medicines words inside
This wind

Hi niswas vita ki ni

We shall live again..........

Feb 7..04
Bologna

Crossings

There are shadows moving inside the arriving light

Drifting across the horizons of everything
Edges of grief
Edges of desire

There is nothing to remember that has not imagined us

Our broken wings

Our shimmering days

11.26.03
Bologna

Elf

                                                                To my daughter

In the presence of these days
Among roads of glistening moons and songs

I have opened a window
Wide enough to see you arriving
Small droplets of a star on you face

The scent of a grass wind on your fingertips

We have lain together while the music of the world passed
The light coming out of your breath standing in the frozen trees

Chrystalline forms of faces on the whitened leaves
See how you have awakened them
Each one looking at you from a wounded sleep

Their small wings shimmering

Ready to fly……

For Zoe, Hostonohon
12.11.04

For the child killed in Bethlehem by Israeli soldiers

again it is the middle of night
again there is the scent of blood in the rivers

and a broken hand holding a candle
and a drinking cup of one who can no longer drink

and in Bethlehem the shadow of a child that
can no longer stand up

the trembling song of a bird
and its screaming message that is not its own

waiting for us…

Unter Hueb, Switzerland
feb 22.03

From Jordan

At the hotel Sadeen the heat burns into my skin
Sitting on a small veranda
Facing a busy street
It is morning and on the stifling Bedouin wind
The bodies of dead Iraqi children sail by
In an array of swirling birds

Their dreams settle around me whispering
The tiniest words
The ones not even the terror of war could tear
From their souls

Down a small road a boy riding a donkey
Dismounts
Searching through the garbage of a dumpster

I close my eyes
Searching for the torn garment of a prayer
I found once in Oklahoma among the damp autumn leaves
Along a river....

Jordan
9.15.05

Here is the snow that has fallen for three days
Here the quiet hours before dawn

We reach out of the past
Walking among silent things

As long as we can

What lies at the end of the hour
A child's ring on the dark table
Sunflowers broken
By the rain

All the wild things resting beside the edges of our lives

Their feet made of glass...

May 17.05

I have followed you

Not knowing who you were

The clear scent of autumn in your hair
A gull drifts over the lake toward the rest of its life
It has come a long way

It has brought it only song

Everywhere the vanishing continues
Even here

Yet in the darkness someone is praying

Silence standing by the trees
In the rain

Como, Italy, for Silvana
11.23.02

I sat with doomed angels under a tree in a luminous rain

I sat with doomed angels under a tree in a luminous rain
All night wolf spirits smelled my hair and skin

Following the one obsession given me by my grandfathers my grandmothers
Crossing into the borderlands
Where the charred handwriting of someone else
Falls into my own

The way back a weary thread of light

Strands of dawn moved gently the leaves
I stood
Took a piss
And tasted water from the sky....

Dog soldier poem in exile
In the Swiss mountains

5 august 05

Sunlight moved inside the thousand specks of dust
In a cheap hotel in Tijuana
Your cigarette smoke awoke me
Pulsing toward the half opened window

You were never there

The blood on the whiskey bottle was mine

Years later I have still the words you gave me
Thank you

I have gone toward those who are lost
And found your footprints

Even at the edge
Of nothing…..

For my uncles

August 1,05
Icici, Croatia

In a Slovakia hotel

Past midnight through the open window there was your voice
A tremoring calling from a distance too far to reach

I walked outside to a deserted street

I stood in a shattered phone booth in a frozen wind

Later watching shadows upon the wall

 you were there
Standing on a long bridge alone

Outside the window
Moonlight falling upon another war....

For my brother Mike
12 march 07

In a vagrant winter wind
All the earths gentleness hiding in the leaves

Leaves waiting in their long silences
Leaves covering our shame
Leaves shining on our closed faces

And on this solemn journey among the loneliest of us

Hand-prints falling out of a female rain....

Netzchkau, Germany
3 October 06

In the fog of these Swiss mountains i turn
From the indifference of war

Building a small fire
Sitting awhile among wind and rain

Far from the varied ignorance of men

I sit among the ones lost in the infinite
Their poet voices rising from the mass graves
Of Kosovo and wounded knee

Their country a bleeding wound that cannot contain them

They have placed their lives in front of pain and sorrow

Turning toward what is left
Of the light....

Lines above the snowline
22 April 06

Journeying with Basho

From far downriver the echoes of cities

You are returning and there are no sweet winds
To hold you
No fields to hear you remembering
Not even the pale moon
That once remembered everything

Outside the window the light is moving away
The tracks of animals holding themselves for the last time

The gathering night full of stillness....

We have waited a long time
In our prayers we have lit lamps though the words
That know us have turned away

Others without the hope of prayer
Have walked through our bodies and lain down

Their voices fallen into the rivers....

I search the long daylight of winter

I hold what i can see
As one holds someone who is going away

Tomorrow no one will know this
Has happened

No one will remember....

Awakening from the distant screaming
On the streets of Kosovo and Kabul

Names rise up in a misted rain
They put their hands upon our eyes
That have grown lonely and searching

In this torn place
A leaf falls leaving its shadow
On the wind and the birds in their songs....

Just after midnight in the Denver bus station
I ask a shoeshine black man where the Indian bars are

We walk outside and he points toward the rounded moon
Soule street he whispers

Three blocks away i find Soule street
And a red neon bar sign with the r shot out
Inside Merle haggard sings mama tried

I settle in and order a 25 cent beer lighting a Toscanello
And old man behind the bar watching
I'm sitting next to a midget
His legs dangling beneath him
Wearing little boy tennis shoes
He asks me for a cigar

They call me the prophet he says
I didn't think they called you slim I said
People keep buying him beers and he slides
a few my way

a Mexican and an Indian start a fight over a toothless
babe with nice legs
guns and knives everywhere

the barman shouts a beer for everyone
the fight stops
I see him staring at the whirling ceiling fan

I have owned this bar for 56 years he says to me

I smile and descend into a dark winged price
already paid
drinking warm beer with these bruised eyes and souls

entering the backside of a song
another beer sliding in front of me

Denver
jan10.04

Soule street, name for the army capt Silas soule who testified against col.
Chivington, the officer who ordered the massacre of Cheyennes at sand creek,1864

Merle Haggard..country music singer

Where am I waiting for you
streets soaked in voices
the coffee cup fills with rain

the Paris sky grey orange
I walked into what ever light there was
through small alleyways
filled with forgotten names

in the Chimbu highlands
with Papua New Guinea poets in a tin shack
we read poems
after they shared their last bread with me
our words touching us quietly
into the deep night

soon after awakening
I remembered dreaming of a field of white skulls
in Rwanda
the only darkness
the holes where their eyes were

this San Francisco morning
I remember the war that is here
and inside a sail of wind
the great memory that waits
wanting to cross over
from the other side

Amy Kimberleys apt
1-23-96

In the memorized things within me
Rain falling upon the mountains
Of eastern Oklahoma

On a dark road i passed the body of a dead
angel

Its loose wing lifting and falling
In a strong wind at the side of the road....

June9.06

Between our arms
The breathing world continues
Past the bandages hung out to dry
And the dark hair that hangs from the trees

Between our arms there are winds from the wars
Passages upon footpaths
Two deep to contain words

In sleep I saw animals moving toward the sea
They were all the names of the missing

When I awoke there were your hands
Waiting at the edge
Of everything....

Silvana poems
27jan03

Poem from ammon

Too far the jester whispered as I landed from Bavaria
How far is that I wrote on the dust on the table
The dragon lady with a dark pen scribbling my face
On the desert wind

And all the words I used on the telephone
Could not spell your name

Eating meat on a road near the airport
Under the Pleiades
Desert cops with friendly guns arrived
Shook hands and drove off
Toward the war inside their minds

Seven dogs in mythic masks appeared from a sacred hole
In the universe
The two that would not leave are with me now
Their eyes shine in the rains that hover over the human
Shit storm

Moonlight sitting with the Cheyenne tobacco prayers
Under the tomb
Of a fallen king...

Jordan..9.15.05

Rain songs

Birds sitting in the silent trees

The bones of your hands
Full with disappearing faith

We are calling toward a place where
Someone is standing
Someone who remembers

Small hands opening in sleep
Filling with moonlight

The last words of a language
Praying for us

Vihomiv tsido ehemin eneh histai..

Look at this one singing toward his heart..

July4.05

What is this shadow-play
Dark silhouettes that move
Against each other
Upon a bordered wall

On CNN a child without a face
Moves from side to side
In a crib in Sarajevo

Outside this window
Two dragons atop a pagoda

Are fighting over the moon

9.16.93/11.27.93
Singapore

Seventeen lines

For my son Michael

I have wandered toward eyes that have long been closed
And border-towns that would not leave me alone

I am following your footprints out of a memory

Here in my sixty first year
Nothing is clearer or more beautiful than your face

I walked toward the darkened houses
Looking for a candle on a window ledge
Something you told me years ago when i held you

Where ever you are
You will not dream alone

Look for me

I write your name

On anything i can find

17may.05

Silvana

Wind soft against the white curtains
in this room
Catalan voices enter the streets and alleyways
a small boy is carrying dried fruit
fallen from the moon

last night in a Barcelona bar I tasted the absence
of you
calling toward you now
the cries of the vanished less loud behind my eyes

since i found you....

Barcelona
June 11,05

From this place lit by the snow
Nothing is moving
The house with its east window and the morning star

Here is a solemnity
That cannot turn away from itself
And will never be the same
Because you have moved within it

Against the fatigue of another dawn
You arrive in a quiet voice
Offering a hand full of salt
You found in a forest at the edge of a dream

The silence of snowfall at 3 a m
The window open to the cold air

A letter on the table
Its words written in a memoried autumn

Of a life escaped into the wind....

Gibswil-reid
Switzerland
12.6.99

1

arriving in late afternoon
silence hanging from the fishing nets

now the half moonlight glistens on the trees

so many frontiers to cross
the shadows of so many on one side
their silenced bodies on the other

I find solace in the small hand that fits into
my own

a birds voice falls into the darkened leaves …

2

I remember a hard rain falling on the futureless harbor
a ship filled
with insinuating eyes and tired languages.

near midnight a dog barks at a wildness
that simply watches
and stars whose lights
refuse to die
long after their breath has disappeared … …

4.26.02

waiting near dawn
here is my voice that cannot sing to you

this way is the way to the sea
we will be there
when the shattered glass and soundless bells

drift ashore from Albania

the broken animals and broken trees
looking back from the same place with the same eyes

humans are the only ones who pray for themselves ... ...

4.26.02

early summer
small owls are sitting where the moon will pass
between two willow trees

a bell ringing near midnight

in Bethlehem the same bell sounds
over the starving
and forsaken
the faithless and the faithfull

wings of light and tears flying away

the mirrors are full of hands and prayers reaching out
from the other side
so near

no one believes what they see
so they live

in a remembered sorrow ... ...

4.29.02

waiting for the moon.. i rest with your name in my hands..
you are sleeping now.. far from the doors of snow..
the chaff of the moon fills the valley.. with its flowers of sea wind and its gloves that
have let go the fallen..
i take into my breath their names their hopes..when you awaken I will give them to
you ... ...

live with your hands open to hold the ones no one remembers.. in remembrance of
their voices their eyes.. each day the empty cups from which they drank will be a
river from which you can drink.. and you will never be alone ... ...

4.30.02
Casa castiglioncello
San Martino
Isola di Elba

Here is the long night
Splintering over the fields
A whitened hair of memoried hours
Falls out of the moonlight

My mothers hands reach across the table
Into another time
Where the rain moved without clocks
And no one was left behind

Here is what is left and what shall never be
Sitting as a dark bird at our windows

I awoke in the middle of night
A shadowy child watching from the corner
Of the room

Feathers from the rain had fallen
Into his mouth

All the gates were left open
Once again night flaring scarlet
Behind my eyes...

El Reno, Oklahoma
Jan 16,04

Trilogy on an Italian train

For Danielle Militic

We watched out the train window
Our faces brushing the nights landscape
That passed
In its hurried way beyond the glass
Somewhere in Italy
Your notebook a shimmering voice of passion
In your words
Whispering as only the hunted can whisper

It is the darks own leaping
Out of our mouths
From under our shoes
In the pieces of light in a dense forest
And we learn to say goodbye
To the things we love

It is still winter in your voice she said
I lit a cigar and watched the worlds sadness
Drifting through her eyes

In America at the edge of a freeway
A man is holding a torn cup filled with darkness

It is a kind of darkness i have seen before

Bosnian girl, age 19, I met on a train escaping
The war in ex Yugoslavia, may 21,1992.. upon
Returning she went missing in 1993....

Wind and sunlight near twelve mile point

Wind and sunlight near twelve mile point

And you are there gathering cedar
Under a day moon

Years ago i flung my name into this water

Now this dusklight grown deep inside my memory

Tastes of loss...

A calumet poem
11.10.02

for my grandfather

woheiv
do sah ni vistoh

morning star
what do you see….

You have known where the moon was
In your sleep it was there
In your breath
In your eyes that were traveling

From Darfur and new Orleans from Kosovo to
Guantanamo

there is a singing water
where their names rise up

In a misted rain they put their hands
In our tracks

Praying for us

As from this torn place
A leaf falls
Leaving its name on the wind

The day made of thin glass breaking
Through our names

Through our hearts

A birds faint calling far away

A dream of a tattered red cloth falling to earth
But whose dream

All the sorrowed voices falling away
And the edge of everything

To move in open country

To sit in a clear place

To guard life....

Dog soldier prayer
Cheyenne

Table of contents

Printed by Books on Demand GmbH, Norderstedt / Germany